Les Très Riches Heures

with Poems
by
Tony Whedon

Fomite
Burlington, Vermont

Copyright 2017 © by Tony Whedon

All rights reserved. No part of this book may be reproduced in any form or by any means without the prior written consent of the publisher, except in the case of brief quotations used in reviews and certain other noncommercial uses permitted by copyright law.

Tony Whedon is the author of two previous books of poetry. His poems and essays appear in Harpers, American Poetry Review, Iowa Review, Prairie Schooner, Sewanee Review, Ploughshares and over a hundred other literary magazines. His essay collection A Language Dark Enough won the Mid-List Press award for Creative Non-Fiction. He lives with his wife Suzanne in Montgomery, Vermont.

ISBN-13: 978-1-944388-30-0

Fomite
58 Peru Street
Burlington, VT 05401
www.fomitepress.com

Les Très Riches Heures

Introduction

Is there a real subject for elegy? We readily identify it with the neo-classical ruins of Lorraine and Ruisdael, the weeping landscapes of the English Romantics, the rhapsodic vistas of the Hudson River School -- paintings that turn to us the sublime face of elegy and make us regret the loss of the natural world. Virgil's Eclogues lament the displacement of small farmers by the Roman government from their land as a reward to the military. The enclosures acts of the English 18th century provoked painters and poets to elegize a freer pastoral life. Likewise, 19th century American artists and writers compose elegies to an Eden displaced by steam engines and locomotives. But the brothers Herman, Paul, and Johan Limbourg, 1385 – 1416 who in the early fifteenth century created the miniatures in this little book express a more complex set of grief. At the direction of their inspired patron, Jean, the Duke of Berry, they mourn the loss of a feudal order, grieve for a stable agrarian world. The paintings also reflect a desire to escape the painful distractions of politics through art. An undertow of renunciation flows through them. We observe it in the doleful expressions of the peasants in March, October and December (You don't need to be an historian to note the brutal effect of feudalism in the Très Riches Heures) whose emotion is more wistful than lamentative, whose figures don't quite know what they mourn for, nor do they seem aware that they mourn; we see it, too, in the muted, almost translucent tones of mid-summer cutting and September harvest.

The elegy depends on idealized memory moments – in the Limbourgs' case, on fairytale versions of what the immediate past was like. Was the feudal order of the late-Middle Ages as discretely contained as the Limbourgs' miniatures depict it? Was the sky such a brilliant shade of blue, the maidens so absurdly lovely? The figures we meet here, conceived at the early beginning of the French Renaissance, are not yet flesh-and-blood; they've not quite assumed individuality, much less personality or human form.

The creators of the Très Riches Heures, grew up in the town

of Nimragen in the duchy of Guelden between the Meuse and the Rhine. Their father was a wood sculptor. The Meuse region they came from was renowned for its goldsmiths and miniaturists, and as adolescents the brothers were goldsmith apprentices in Paris. Sculptural elements of the Limbourgs' paintings are hinted at in the volume of their free-standing figures and in their chiseled shapeliness, their balanced occupation of space. As goldsmiths, the brothers would have learned about the resistance of inert materials and about minute figuration and ornamentation, manifested later in their paintings by their intricate detailing and by the implied weight of their figures. In 1410 the brothers installed themselves with Duke Jean de Berry. The following year Paul gave to the Duke a facetious New Year's gift -- "a counterfeit made of wood with no pages and nothing written within" covered with white velvet and adorned with a vermeil clasp. Gifts were exchanged between the duke and the Limbourgs over a long period, the most interesting a salt-cellar encrusted with gold Paul gave to the duke which may be the same appearing in the month of January in the Très Riches Heures. The Limbourgs created another book of miniatures, The Très Belles Heures of Jean, the Duke of Berry, to be found in New York's Cloisters, whose subject matter doesn't engage me as do the Très Riches Heures; and most of their other work is lost.

To the French duke, the Limbourgs' sponsor, they were northerners, but not northern northerners, occupying, as Flemish artists, a geographical middle-land. Their landscapes are commodious but not lush; their slender women a little pot-bellied. Despite their pastoral themes, in some paintings the peasants look weary. It's anyone's guess if the artists intended the peasants to look like they were suffering, but history tells us that the French countryside during a time of plague, war and the break-up of the nobility's estates was affected by a huge drop in the population.

While other artists of the time interpreted these dramatic changes as signs of the apocalypse, the Duke of Berry and the brothers Limbourg responded with an art of elegiac sweetness made poignant by their seasonal themes. The two parts to The Très Riches Heures consist of twelve calendar paintings of the four seasons and illustrated extracts from the New Testament. The religious paintings are accompanied by texts in red Gothic calligraphy. The calendar pictures in the Très Riches Heures of Jean, Duke of Berry found here have no reference to religious matters -- not one Christian icon appears in the work. Fairytale chateaux tower over laboring peasants; a striking blue horoscope with gold planets and God on his throne (more a Roman God than Christian) rules the heavens, and a naive delight suffuses the paintings.

The division of labor in the Limbourg paintings emphasizes what we already know: that while the peasantry worked, and worked very hard, the nobility played very hard. The yeomanry is depicted in demure – if idealized – outfits, and the nobility sport the latest in late-Medieval high fashion. While the rites of May focuses on the nobility, another equestrian miniature, the month of August, more fully represents the division between aristocrats and peasants.

The Duke of Berry, who came along three centuries after Mont St. Michel was built, was a collector of just about everything. As brother of King Charles V, the duke owned large tracts of land in central France, but his appetite for things exotic left him in the poor house. His eclectic taste included a passion for historiated tapestries, Luccan gold brocade, silk wall hangings, porcelains, and gold-inlaid forks and spoons; his assortment of rubies and precious stones rivaled any in Europe. The duke accumulated a zoo of bears, ostriches and dromedaries, and a kennel of Pomeranians. He assembled a library of sumptuously bound books that included 41 secular histories, 38 chivalric romances, three maps of the world, a book of divination, an astrological treatise on the seven planets, fourteen bibles, sixteen psalters, six missals; a copy of Gossun's Imago Mundi and Le Livre de la Sphere, by Nicholas Oresme, Fleures des Histoires de la Terre Orien, and Marco Polo's account of his expeditions to China.

Jean de Berry was born on November 30, 1340, third son of Jean II, Le Bon. He'd have been happy left to his indulgences, but at the end of his life, forced into politics, he played a conciliatory role in negotiations with the English and helped end for a time the schism that divided western Christianity. In his seventies, the duke saw the peace disturbed by a rivalry between the houses of Burgundy and Orleans. In 1411 the Hôtel de Nesle, his Paris palace, was ransacked and his Chateau de Bicêtre near the city was pillaged and burned. The next year he was besieged in Bourges, the capital of Berry, by the Burgundians, and in 1413 the extremes of the Cabochien movement forced him to take refuge in the Cloister de Notre Dame. The Duke had just recouped from all this when the French were again at war with England which ended in the tragic French defeat at Agincourt in 1415.

The tone of The Book of Très Riches Heures, commissioned at this time, no doubt was influenced by Jean's disillusionments. What better way to forget the plots and sub-plots of royal family feuds and the violent theological hair-splitting of rival church factions than to lose oneself in Arcadia? In the last ten years of his life, the Limbourgs at his side, the duke directed page by page the illustration of his two books of hours. The miniatures in the Très Riches Heures were painted, save for half of September and all of November, by the Limbourgs. We don't know the extent to which the duke's taste affected the paintings, but their austere calm suggests someone at the contemplative end of his days.

All three brothers died in 1416, not yet in their mid-thirties. They are thought to have been victims of the plague. Jean de Berry died in the same year. Less than a decade after their deaths, many of the estates in these miniatures were burned to the ground by the English and were overgrown with saplings.

~~~~~~~~~~

I've known these paintings since childhood from a book of Limborg reproductions my artist mother had in her library. Her own drawings and watercolors and painted tiles (she specialized in the latter) evoked with their pastoral detail a world not unlike the one in Très Riches Heures. In the dining room of our little Cape Cod house, she did pen-ink sketches she copied onto tiles of Central Park and scenes from the bayou country where she grew up.

Back then these minatures appealed to me as they do now. I related to their nature scenes, to their pure pageantry and brightly colored regalia. They were unthreatening; there was no war, no crucifixion, no apotheosizing clutter of saints and sinners, and they presented a clear narrative based on human experience and the progression of the seasons.

The spaciousness of the scenes gave my imagination room to wander.

JANUARY

Second Watch. Cold moonlight slices through
the Limbourg's skulls. First the primaries,
Paul says, blue to Jean de Berry's robe, and
crimson and cardinal red to a priest's
vestments, a diner's medallioned jacket.
There's wine and more wine, iced oysters
from Normandy soaking in brine;
roasted sparrows the size of thimbles;
fresh dug turnips and candied beets on
on a damask tablecloth laid with
platters, plates and a gold saltcellar.

"Look, look," Paul murmurs to his
brother who turns slowly to the princes
and lackeys in a midnight draft of
January. Their eyes tear up. These two
love each other like brothers; they love how
a New Years feast is sumptuously
transformed. To the left, someone tips a flagon,
and behind him a tapestry of knights
(out of Uccello) cue up their horses to
meet the enemy. In his fluffy
fur hat, the duke keeps the wine coming.

Nobles clothed in linens, elaborate
head pieces, a priest officiating in
a red and gold surplice – who are they
waiting for? The Duke's puppies roam the table,
plundering the choice cuts of venison.
Behind, a hearth fire is protected by
a fanned wicker screen. None of this keeps
Death, a bitter winter's death by plague
or overeating, from inserting
Himself into this sparkling miniature.
Outside the chateau's gates come the cries of the poor.

FEBRUARY

A mantle of sea-gray blue drifts
through the Normandy forests, a blue
smuggled in satchels from Istanbul
and ground with care into paste a half tone
brighter than dawn breaking through the duke's
clerestory window. Winter outside:
two peasants warm themselves by a fire,
tunics pulled up, genitals exposed
to the warmth; beside them, the lady
of the house (in blue) raises her petticoats.
The three gaze past the wattle enclosure
into February. Above the fire,
washrags hang out to dry; behind
their house, more of a hut with its straw
chimney and flimsy straw roof, brandy casks,
corn husks, nine rooks feeding on scraps by
the sheepfold. This winter morning
Paul recalls his mother, her face stricken
black, screaming "Fire!" He ran with
a bucket to the village well, and when
he returned, the house had gone down,
the last timbers guttering. What a fire does,
how it leaps and sputters, has terrified him
ever since. Now the snow is no longer
snow; a quiet comes in eddies
in an event marked on the calendar
and briefly marveled at by a man in white
trousers and blue shirt waist splitting wood.
Behind him, to his left, a peasant
drives a donkey toward a town all but smudged
out by falling snow. Market day deep
in winter's hush, and all this slips into
invisibility — even time
and the sad lack of it. Bees doze in their hives;
the villagers sleep till another
northern spring awakes them.

MARCH

Of course one wants to show more than a little
pity for one's subjects, but don't, dear Paul,
make them so pitiful that they detract
from the scene. And so humble and drab
they upstage the first groping of spring.

An old man follows two oxen along
the winter bleached grass. He looks smart in
his trimmed white beard, gray stockings, black bootlets
and gray surcoat — a splash of crimson at his waist
might be a pocket or a purse. Smoke

from the Chateau Lusignan's kitchen
chimney stains the Breton sky; then the turrets,
the two enceinte, and below the chateau gates
sixteen sheep, a shepherd, a bounding sheep dog,
a fattened ewe, carry one high up

the castle walls. But who knows the ploughman's
story and why should we care?
A collector of silly miniatures
meant not to instruct but to entertain,
a lover of obscure texts and oriental

pigments, a breeder of dogs and trader
of horses, the duke can't ignore
the ruin closing around him. Three peasants
trim grape vines in an enclosure,
a fairy named Melusine turns into

a winged dragon on Saturdays and
flutters over the Tour Melusine,
a gold escutcheon of a dragon.
Metamorphosis after metamorphosis
winter into a muddy spring, a peasant

into a ploughman prince. Labor into
more labor. Tonight bright pennants fly
over the ramparts. War cries echo within.

APRIL

Just eleven! But pretty girls ought to die young
"Young as April," Charle's d'Orleans,
prince, poet and the Duke's soon to be grandson,
says about the girl with her hand extended
in this betrothal scene on the broad lawn
of his chateau at Dourdan: seven of them,
including the young couple, two maidens
picking violets in sculpted gowns,
the mother, black robed in a gold hat,
and the duke's own son in a flat topped black tuque.
An engagement party, early spring,
the prince in a fleecy pompadour
of a hat he, a ruby crowned kinglet,
and the bride to be pale as a blue jay.
No angel consecrates the scene, not even
a pagan cupid. Everything's tri-
angulated by a chateau with
its own bronze crown and the right angles of
an orchard's enclosure, by the Riviere Orge
with two fishing boats on it, so peaceful
save for a horoscope that foretells, if we
read it right, a dim future. It's all
so still, love and its accomplices.
In the light of his gaunt windows,
the duke reads a snatch of Dante, a verse
or two from Cavalcanti, but neither
love or art changes things. Jean de Berry,
let these two be happy for now.
The brothers are riding home in
the exacting starlight. Such quarreling
over little things — the shape of a hand,
the gaze of a girl into a young
man's eyes — and yet they're happy.
Some men think these days that art is no more
than a stuffed carcass with devils dancing
on it; but the brothers Limbourg know different.
They are not yet at the end of their days.
Paul says good night and beds down with the horses.

MAY

Girls in green robes and brilliant brocade —
one kerchiefed in white astride a prancing
white horse; two others — her retinue? —
in damasked gold caps evoke the floralia
of antiquity. The Duke wears a flower strewn cape.
He turns on his brindled horse to the girls
who follow the parade through the countryside
to bring back branches. The young gelding
beneath him tugs at the reins; and then
the trembling poplars, and the duke, his mind
elsewhere (lost in revenge?) and the girls,
with half smiles, eyes downcast, riding
with him into the mild afternoon.

A flute, trombone and trumpet lead the group
along the forest's edge past the Palais
de la Cite outside Paris. Its towers
rise behind the trees — each with a cloud crest:
in the dungeon, meanwhile,
someone rattles his cold chains, a rat
rummages across a woman's face.
Chimneys puff wanly into the still air.
The Duke's little dogs romp just short of
the horses' hooves. Everything's stained
and gilded for the Duke who'll pore over
these miniatures one winter day,
an old dog at his feet, dried flowers pressed
and still fragrant between the gold pages.

JUNE

No shadows are cast in most Limbourg paintings,
no footprints left to show where the peasants
touch the ground — they glide above the earth,
without expression, consumed as they are
by cutting and raking. Outside the painting
a baby cries, the Duke sips his frothy
cup of wine. In mid distance three male
reapers wield scythes, and in the foreground
a woman in a pale blue dress holds
a rake, another a twin tined pitch fork,
all this under the same sun that shines
on the slate rooftops of the Palais
de la Cite, on the reapers in flimsy
tunics and blue dresses whose day
begins with a cup of broth and a sigh,
a plunge into the Seine to wash off
dusty sleep, and then the long barefoot
walk to the meadow where hay is cut
and stacked under a pale sky. Paler skin
grass the color of brine, and the river
with cattails foamy behind a promenade
of sea green plum trees. It's Paris.
Early summer. The first hay cutting.

JULY

One harvester, poised like a dancer,
wears a cone shaped straw hat, a simple shirt
and petits draps that ride just above
his thighs; another bends inelegantly
forward, his sickle raised in time with the others.
A field speckled by devil's paint brush
and daisies. Mid summer. In a nearby meadow
shepherds wrestle a pair of sheep into
their laps. They wield their primitive shears
threateningly. The sheep are mere
approximations of sheep. They look docile,
they look like poodles! A wooden footbridge
leads far right to one of the sparkling
towers, and there's a drawbridge, a chapel.
The fortress, regally crowned by
July's horoscope, is set in ragged
mountains — not as impregnable as
you'd think, "A precious document," scholars
tell us, "of a chateau that no longer
exists." Again — and again — the peasants
labor under a sun that casts no shadows.
Bleating lambs, the stink of freshly laid manure;
roar of the river Clain toward evening.

AUGUST

The lead rider wears a hat with upturned brims,
an ultramarine cloak; on the rump
of his horse a maid in a white trimmed frock
leans slightly forward. Her sleeves are crimson,
the reigns of her horse fringed with blood red
tassels. At first you don't recognize
the swimmers, one woman already undressed,
a second naked swimmer — male or female? —
emerges to her left while another floats,
almost submerged, on his back. Bodies grayed
and refracted by murky pond water,
hunters in full regalia, all of them
so stone faced they hardly seem alive,
neither casting a thought at the other.

The brothers work patiently stroke after stroke
under the flicker of sweating candles —
Paul, the elder, whistles a madrigal
and Raoul mutters a prayer to Anthony,
prince of lost things. A falconer with
a hawk on his elbow leads the way —
he drags a long stick. Two birds are released
into a late August evening, the harvest
going on beneath a deepening sky
into which they rise, not much bigger than
barn swallows. Paul squints his tired eyes:
over the corner towers of the Chateau
Saumur's dungeon, the little hawks fly,
keen eyes awake to a fading landscape.

SEPTEMBER

Poor Jean Colombe — compared to the Limbourgs
he's not much of a painter. Grapes are gathered
in purple bunches, dumped into baskets
and wagon vats, then carted off. In

the center foreground a donkey pricks up
his ears and behind him a peasant leans
over, revealing thick buttocks and thighs
a crude, tasteless gesture, but nevertheless real.

The lower half of this split painting
(the confectionary Chateau Saumur
is by the Limbourgs, the grape pickers
by Colombe many years later)

is awash in muddled greens and browns. The crude,
round faced, short waisted peasants tug us
away a moment from the Limbourgs'
timid sweetness. "Colombe no doubt

worked over a sketch by the Limbourgs,"
we're told, "since miniatures were completely
and lightly drawn before being painted."
It's the lightness we miss, a transparent

lightness. (Paul studied in Rome awhile,
and came back knowing how to shape figures,
to make them both ethereal and
filled out with flesh.) But Colombe's grape pickers –

they're more like peasants, sturdier and
hard working. The months come and go. The grapes
bleed into the pickers' hands; their knees hurt
from bending, rising up and sitting down.

OCTOBER

Below the towering Hotel de Nesle,
at the bulls eye of October's miniature,
a scarecrow dressed like an archer

draws his bow. He wears a blue scarf.
His field's already planted
with winter rye, and strings tied to sticks

discourage birds from eating the seeds.
For the first time in the Limbourgs' paintings,
we see footprints and a pale shadow cast by

a sower in a blue smock. A white seed bag drapes
his shoulders. To the left, a black tunicked
peasant on a brown horse drags a harrow

weighted with a stone. Rooks gather only
a few feet from the horse — famished, bunched
and scattered. The duke is inconsolable.

Nothing here says happiness: the sower
is particularly grim; the whites
of his eyes, his furrowed forehead, his

tiny halting steps, even the way he
holds his cupped palm filled with seeds, is dreary.
Save us, Dear Lord, from the hunger of

the winter months to come. The duke
mops his forehead and feels in his pocket
for the copper amulet. It's Paris

again, sowing time under Libra and Scorpio,
and who is the better for it?

NOVEMBER

Nothing tells a story better than a hog.
What it eats and what it wants — a cool pond to
wallow in, a fencepost to scratch its bristled
butt on. In late fall, a hog wants to fatten up.
Regardez, hogs, it's raining fist sized acorns!
But none look up. A chateau's fairy tale
crenellations tell us these hogs come
with a history, blueblood hogs that go back
to the tusked, razorbacks of Charlemagne.
A swineherd flings a stick into an oak's
branches. His left arm falls back in a salute
to November. Oak leaves in the dusk,
peasants with clubs retreating into
a dark oak forest. As their voices
ride down the valley, more hogs rush from
their pens, eyes slanted, and more acorns
patter onto the hogs' heads. Circe
turned Odysseus' shipmates into pigs.
They snuffled around her courtyard
hoping to be changed back into men.
Wake up, hogs! Raise up your heads!
In these last precious hours
your real life is about to begin.

DECEMBER

It's too late for the boar to retreat
into the Forest of Vincennes. Too late!
The dogs plunge into the boar's haunches.
A broad faced man grapples with the tangle
of dogs and holds back a bloodhound whose
tongue lolls from his mouth like a red flag.
The suppleness of the dogs, the way their bodies
contract and ripple — each finds a haunch,
a loin, to gnaw on. And as for the men,
they're not worth much more to the Limbourgs
than a few centimes in the hands of the poor.
But they are men alive to how the leaves
rattle in the wind and alert to when
the dogs catch a scent and begin their
feverish baying. The hunters' bellies
rumble with cold porridge, their armpits
exude an angry stench. Once they were held
by mothers who caressed them, who asked a priest
to bless them, and sent them into this world.
Look how life has changed them. Thanks be to Ovid --
he's left us countless ways to see our world
transformed, fish to bird, bicuspid to crab,
snake into the flaming staves of our pens.
One man with the face of the sower we met
in October (he has yellow patches on his green
britches) curses while another blows
the "mort" on a little horn. The trees
are stained in pale russets, December
light streaks the forest floor. A cold morning,
with no snow. Bloodhounds, boarhounds, their teeth
sunk into a wild pig in a tableau vivant
of rippling dogs, gawking men. A wild boar
bleeds from his mouth. His breath comes fast.
His little hocks, his exquisite tusks.

Thanks to Fomite Press and Suzanne Dollois for her helping me assemble this little book, and to Suzanne Whedon for brightening the calendar of my days.

www.ingramcontent.com/pod-product-compliance
Lightning Source LLC
Chambersburg PA
CBHW042233090526
44588CB00001B/7